ANCIENT B!SON

ASHLEY GISH

ICE AGE CREATURES X BOOKS

NORTH AMERICA

EUROPE

ASIA

AFRICA

SOUTH AMERICA

AUSTRALIA

CREATIVE EDUCATION · CREATIVE PAPERBACKS

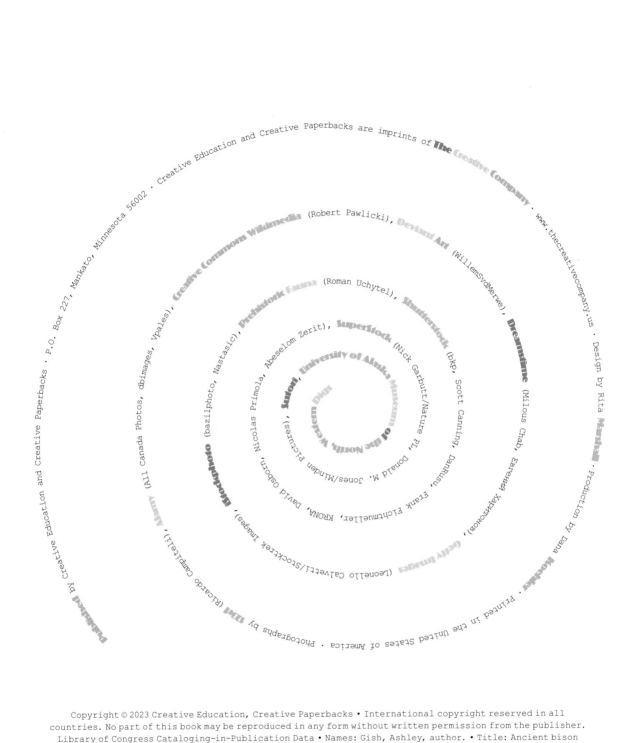

Published by Creative Education and Creative Paperbacks • P.O. Box 227, Mankato, Minnesota 56002 • Creative Education and Creative Paperbacks are imprints of The Creative Company • www.thecreativecompany.us • Design by Rita Marshall • Production by Dana Kocktar • Printed in the United States of America • Photographs by t1zt (Ricardo Campitelli), Alamy (All Canada Photos, dbimages, Vpales), iStockphoto (bazilphoto, Nastassic), Prehistoric Fauna (Roman Uchytel), Creative Common Wikimedia (Robert Pawlicki), Deviant Art (WillemSvdMerwe), Dreamtime (Milous Chab, Евгений Харитонов), Shutterstock (bkp, Scott Canning, Damirux, Frank Fichtmueller, KRONA, David Osborn, Nicolas Primola, Abeselom Zerit), Superstock (Nick Garbutt/Nature PL, Donald M. Jones/Minden Pictures), Getty Images (Leonello Calvetti/Stocktrek Images), Sukovi, University of Alaska Museum of the North, Western Hunt

Library of Congress Cataloging-in-Publication Data • Names: Gish, Ashley, author. • Title: Ancient bison / by Ashley Gish. • Series: X-books: ice age creatures • Includes bibliographical references and index. • Summary: A countdown of five of the most captivating ancient bison fossil discoveries and relatives provides thrills as readers discover more about the biological, social, and hunting characteristics of these Ice Age creatures. • Identifiers: LCCN 2021044482 | ISBN 9781640264328 (library binding) | ISBN 9781628329650 (pbk) | ISBN 9781640006065 (ebook) • Subjects: LCSH: Bison, Fossil—Juvenile literature. • Classification: LCC QE882.U3 G57 2023 / DDC 569/.63—dc23/eng/20211014

ANCIENT B!SON

CONTENTS

ICE AGE CREATURES BOOKS

LONG-HORNED BISON

Bison latifrons

STEPPE BISON

Bison priscus

AMERICAN BISON

Bison bison

XCEPTIONAL ANCIENT ANIMALS

Steppe bison crossed the Bering Land Bridge more than 200,000 years ago. They traveled from Asia to North America. Ancient bison **evolved** from those steppe bison.

Ancient Bison Basics

Ancient bison lived thousands of years ago. They roamed western North America, from Canada to Mexico. They grazed on shrubs and herbs. These animals shared the land with dire wolves, giant ground sloths, mammoths, and other large creatures.

ANCIENT BISON RANGE

NORTH
AMERICA

ANCIENT BISON roamed North America until around 10,000 years ago.

LONG-HORNED BISON SKULL

84 in (213 cm) from tip to tip

STEPPE BISON SKULL

39 in (99 cm) from tip to tip

Ancient bison weighed more than 3,500 pounds (1,587.6 kg). They were nearly seven feet (2.1 m) tall from the bottoms of their hooves to the top of their hump. The muscular hump supported the bison's massive, horned head. They used their head to move snow. They butted heads with hungry predators.

The Wisconsin **Glacial** Episode lasted from about 75,000 to 11,000 years ago. Many large animals either disappeared then or became smaller.

Ancient bison had a layer of coarse guard hairs. This hair kept them dry in rain and snow. Under the guard hairs was soft, warm wool. Ancient bison were rusty red to dark brown. Many bison died around age 10. By that time, their back teeth were worn down. This made it hard for them to eat. The oldest bison were 14 to 16 years old.

Steppe bison could chew tough grasses.

STRONG JAWS

Ancient bison lived during the late Pleistocene epoch. We call it the Ice Age. It lasted from about 2.6 million to 11,700 years ago.

TOP FIVE XTREME ANCIENT BISON

Xtreme Ancient Bison #5

Big Changes Steppe bison came to North America. Then they evolved into two new kinds of bison. These were the ancient bison and the long-horned bison. A glacier began spreading over North America about 75,000 years ago. Steppe bison and long-horned bison could not find enough food. They died out about 20,000 years ago. Ancient bison thrived. They went through more changes. They became smaller and quicker. Today, we know them as American bison.

Ancient Bison Beginnings

Male ancient bison behaved similarly to modern bison. Mating season took place during warm summer months. To show their toughness, males butted heads. The facial bones of males were flatter and wider than those of females. They could withstand smashing into each other. The strongest males mated with females. Size and strength were important traits.

Like modern bison, ancient bison had one baby, called a calf. Calves may have weighed up to 90 pounds (40.8 kg) at birth. A calf could walk and run soon after birth. It had to keep up with the herd. Mothers fed their calves milk. Calves drank milk for about a year. Females reached maturity around age two. Then they had calves of their own. Males did not mate until they were a few years older.

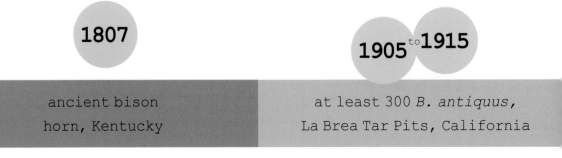

1807

ancient bison
horn, Kentucky

1905 to **1915**

at least 300 *B. antiquus*,
La Brea Tar Pits, California

1954

2003

2009

remains of up to 600 ancient bison, Nebraska

98 bone fragments, Orcas Island, Washington

partial skull, Montana

ANCIENT BISON BEGINNINGS FACT

Many of the remains in the La Brea Tar Pits are from young bison and other creatures such as mammoths.

Xtreme Ancient Bison #4

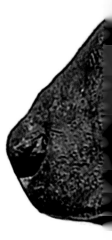

Blue Babe Blue Babe is an Alaskan steppe bison. It died 36,000 years ago. Gold miners found it in 1979. Scratches, bite marks, and even part of a tooth were found on its body. Blue Babe was probably killed by cave lions. Scientists used a bit of the preserved meat to make a stew. The meat was tough, but it didn't taste bad! Blue Babe is on display at the University of Alaska Museum of the North.

XTRAORDINARY LIFESTYLE

Ancient bison lived in groups called herds. They looked like modern bison. But they were bigger, faster, and stronger.

Modern bison are most closely related to cows.

CATTLE COUSINS

BLACK BULL

Ancient Bison Society

Ancient bison are **extinct** members of the Bovidae family. This group includes bison, cattle, sheep, antelope, oxen, and buffalo. Bovids have horns, cloven (divided) hooves, and a four-chambered stomach. The first bovids lived in Asia more than 20 million years ago.

Today, there are 143 different kinds of bovids. Only two are bison. These are the American and European bison, or wisent (*VY-sent*). Humans and bison have lived together for a long time. Humans hunted bison for their meat, hides, bones, and horns. American bison were hunted in large numbers in the 1700s. By 1890, only 1,000 American bison were left in the wild.

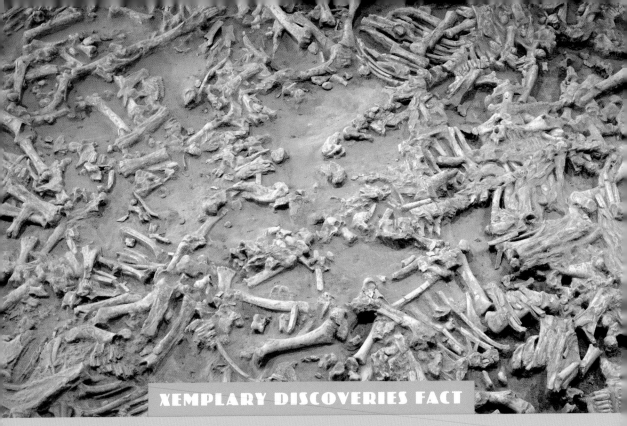

XEMPLARY DISCOVERIES

Scientists study **fossils**. This helps them learn more about what ancient bison looked like. Skull fossils reveal how these animals lived during the Ice Age.

COLD DIRT

Permafrost stays frozen for hundreds or thousands of years.

The bones around the bison's eyes grew longer. This set their eyes out further. This is why researchers think ancient bison had long hair on their faces. The animals had to see past the hair.

Permafrost is soil that stays frozen all the time. Some people have found bison preserved in permafrost. These rare finds often have skin, blood, and hair. Their stomachs may even hold part of the animal's last meal! Remains like these give researchers more clues about what ancient bison looked like and how they lived.

TOP FIVE XTREME ANCIENT BISON

Xtreme Ancient Bison #3

Big Bovid *Bison latifrons*, the long-horned bison, was the largest bison ever to roam North America. It was about eight feet (2.4 m) tall. Its horns, from tip to tip, spread about seven feet (2.1 m) wide. This bison moved slowly. It used its horns for defense. It swatted away predators that jumped on its back. A hungry saber-toothed cat might not have survived a blow from a bison's sharp horns!

XASPERATING CONFLICT

Scientists think humans hunted many animals at the end of the Ice Age. It's possible that human activity was part of the reason that ancient bison died out.

Ancient Bison Survival

For thousands of years, bison were an important source of meat for humans. One way humans hunted bison was by driving them to steep cliff edges. Entire herds of bison were chased over cliffs. At the bottom, hunters killed and processed the bison for food.

Hunters often left bison bones behind. The bones became preserved in soil. These places are known as kill sites. Today, **paleontologists** study kill sites. They learn about ancient bison and other extinct animals.

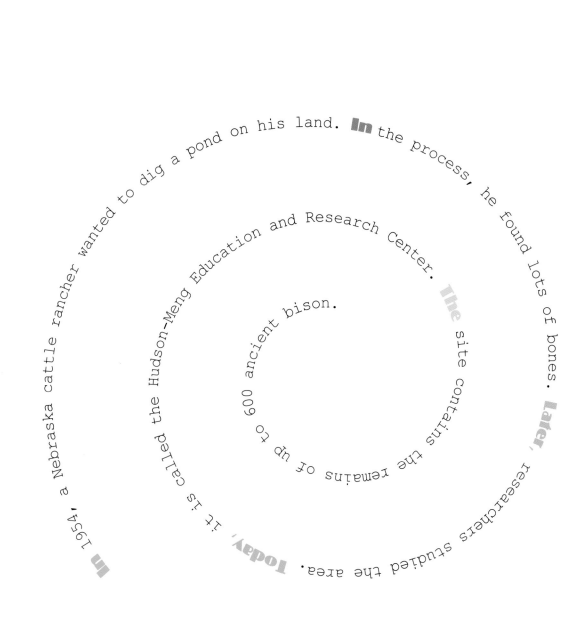

In 1954, a Nebraska cattle rancher wanted to dig a pond on his land. In the process, he found lots of bones. Later, researchers studied the area. Today, it is called the Hudson-Meng Education and Research Center. The site contains the remains of up to 600 ancient bison.

ANCIENT BISON SURVIVAL FACT

Ancient bison were hunted by wolf packs. They developed smaller, lightweight horns so they could outrun wolves.

Xtreme Ancient Bison #2

Rising Numbers European bison descended from steppe bison. They were hunted to extinction in the wild. In the 1950s, conservation groups started breeding European bison living in zoos. They introduced small herds into the wild. Soon the population grew to more than 6,000. They live throughout Europe and Russia. Thanks to successful breeding programs and hunting bans, the bison's numbers continue to rise.

XCITING FACTS

Bison are ruminant animals. They throw up partially digested food into their mouths and continue chewing it.

Some types of bison gave rise to **subspecies**. The two subspecies of American bison are the wood bison and plains bison.

Even though they had big bodies and short legs, ancient bison were fast, agile runners.

Unlike how deer shed their antlers, bison never lose their horns.

The western bison was a smaller bison that evolved from ancient bison about 11,000 years ago. It went extinct about 5,000 years ago.

Male ancient bison were bigger than females. This is also true for modern bison.

Male bison are called "bulls," and females are called "cows."

Bison horns are made of keratin, the same material in human fingernails.

The scientific name for ancient bison is *Bison antiquus*.

The western bison had rearward-pointing horns that were thinner and sharper than other bison's.

Ancient bison probably remained pregnant for about nine months. This is the same length of time as American bison.

American bison are direct descendants of ancient bison.

Bovids are found all across Europe, Africa, Asia, and North America.

Blue Babe was named for the bluish mineral

vivianite that formed on its skin during its preservation in the soil.

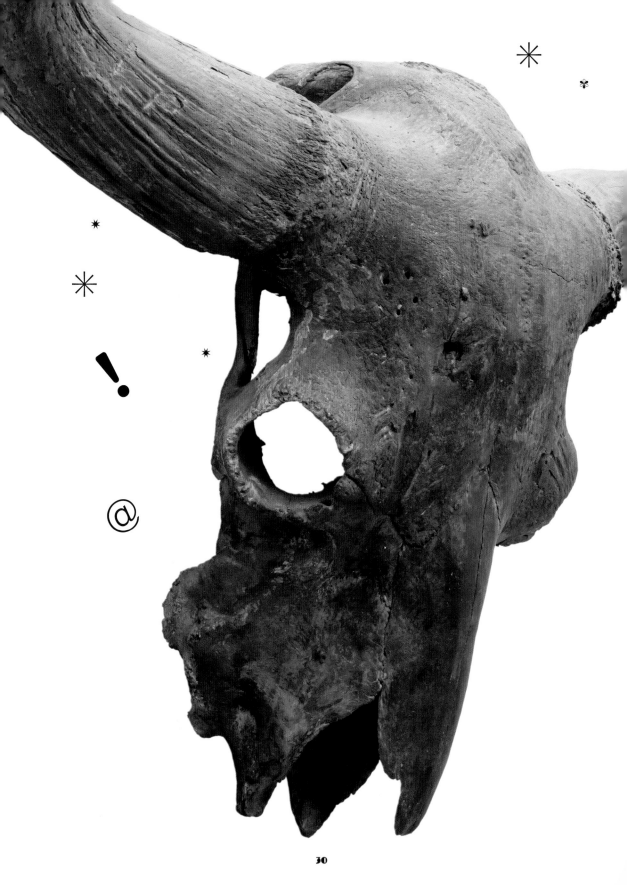

Xtreme Ancient Bison #1

Old Bison, Young Specimen Scientists uncovered an ancient bison skull in Ontario, Canada, in the 1970s. It was just 4,850 years old. Most scientists agree that ancient bison died out about 10,000 years ago. But this bison tells a different story. Some scientists believe small populations of ancient bison survived for thousands of years. They lived in isolated areas. This bison's remains suggest it died of old age.

GLOSSARY

evolved – developed gradually over time into a different form

extinct – having no living members

fossils – the remains of once-living things preserved in rock

glacial – related to a slow-moving mass of ice

paleontologists – scientists who study the fossils of extinct animals

steppe – flat, treeless grassland

subspecies – members within a species that have distinct traits

RESOURCES

Medina, Nico. *What Was the Ice Age?* New York: Penguin Random House, 2017.

Salyer, Hannah. *Packs: Strength in Numbers*. Boston: Houghton Mifflin Harcourt, 2019.

Tite, Jack. *Mega Meltdown: The Weird and Wonderful Animals of the Ice Age*. New York: Blueprint Editions, 2018.

INDEX

Thanks to conservation efforts, about 20,000 American bison are alive today. This is just 1 percent of the estimated bison population before the 1700s.